The Chronicles
of
LOWER PIDDLINGTON

by Stanley Longman

The Chronicles of Lower Piddlington

Copyright¬© 2020 by Stanley Longman
Design Copyright¬© 2020 by Burns Studio Art

All rights reserved. No part of this book may be used or reproduced by any means, graphic, electronic, or mechanical including photocopying, recording, tape or by any information storage retrieval system without the written permission of the publisher except in the case of brief quotations embodied in critical articles and reviews.

Bilbo Books Publishing
www.BilboBooks.com

ISBN- 978-1-7326180-7-7
ISBN- 1-7326180-7-0

Printed in the United States of America

All rights reserved. Published in the United States of America by
Bilbo Books Publishing. Athens, Georgia

To contact Bilbo Books Publishing email
bilbobookspublishing@gmail.com

THE CHRONICLES OF lower Piddlington

*L*ower Piddlington is a village that lies in the foothills of a range of gentle mountains, just south of Greater Piddlington. There is no Lesser Piddlington nor Upper Piddlington, no West or East Piddlington – just two Piddlingtons. There may be some historical or political reason for this arrangement, but if so, it is lost in time.

The villagers are generally good-natured, although they have lapses from time to time. It is a tight-knit community where everyone has at least a nodding acquaintance with everyone else. That also means that they are very curious about strangers who may visit or take up residence in the community. That is certainly true of the Curmudgeon and the Ugly Half-Sister and several others whose stories are told in this collection.

The village is society in miniature, with all its warmth and compassion as well as its prejudices and narrow-mindedness. The arrival of a stranger or the departure of one of their own can trigger those feelings. These chronicles record them:

1. An Incorrigible Curmudgeon
2. The Ugly Half-Sister Comes to Visit
3. The Anxious Page Turner
4. The Transformation of Lugubrious Louie
5. A Squabbling Couple
6. The Town of Babel
7. A Doomsayer Marches in the Streets
8. A Wedding and a Funeral

Lower Piddlington

Greater Piddlington

Concert Hall

Government Building

Landescomb House

...r...eet

Sofie's Window

...olrup House

East Portal

The author dedicates this work to

Charles Embree, a dear departed friend

John Opitz, a life-long friend

Nicolas Coster, a long-time friend

Ursula Vogel, a new friend

Other books by Stanley Longman

Composing Drama for Stage and Screen, 1986

Remus Tales, 1991
(from Joel Chandler Harris)

Theatre Symposium, Vol. 5: Drama as Rhetoric / Rhetoric as Drama: An Exploration of Dramatic and Rhetorical Criticism (Editor), 1997

Theatre Symposium, Vol. 6: Crosscurrents in The Drama: East and West (Editor). 1998

Page and Stage: An Approach to Script Analysis, 2004

Theatre Symposium, Vol. 16: Comedy Tonight!, 2008
(with Jay Malarcher and others)

Corah's Magical Excursions in The Night (Bilbo Books), 2018

Age-Old Tales of The Greeks and Hebrews: Altered, Twisted and Mutilated (Bilbo Books), 2020

The people of Lower Piddlington

A CAST OF CHARACTERS, IN ORDER OF APPEARANCE

Clarence P. Golrup IV
The kid, aka Ralph Morse
Sofia, aka Letitia
Cuthbert Perry
Hilde Baumgartner
Maestro Antonio Benvenuti
Louie Benderbeck
Charlie Gunkle
Pastor Barttleby
Clarissa Landescomb
Mrs. Landescomb, her mother
Wanda Torrance
Will Torrance
The Doomsayer
Max Welbourne
Mayor Geoffrey Bolton
Margaret Murchison, aka Lady Margaret
Jeremy Cogdon
The Sheriff
Mrs. Morse
Mr. Landescomb

An Incorrigible Curmudgeon

Clarence P. Golrup IV was not a happy man. He shared his discontent with whomever he met. Some expressed their wonder if the previous Golrups (I, II, III) were equally given to foul moods. The town wit quipped they couldn't have been and still have begotten a succession of Golrups.

This particular Golrup had come to Lower Piddlington where he took lodging in a house near the central square. He spent much time at the large window, scowling and glaring at the people passing by. People learned to cross to the other side of the street to avoid his glare. That glare was such that whoever caught his eye had the sensation of its boring right into the brain.

It was not only his glare that had an unsettling effect. He spoke with a kind of growl that had a similarly penetrating effect. Naturally, whenever he emerged from his house onto the street, he cut a wide swath as people scurried to get out of his way. That deep growl of his seemed to be saying, "Get out of my way!" And he would push on his rollator, sometimes knocking any person who failed to give way.

Once a week, he would emerge onto the street in order to go to the local post office to pick up his disability check and then to the bank to cash it. On one such day, he was passing the playing field where a group of boys were playing soccer. The ball rolled onto the sidewalk and stopped in front of Clarence Golrup's rollator. Naturally, one of the boys ran after the ball, but came to an abrupt halt when he sensed that infamous glare. For just a few moments they stood there stock-still. Then Golrup lifted the rollator and used it to kick the ball. The ball rolled away and then plummeted down a ravine. He growled and moved on, leaving the poor boy to ponder what to do. His teammates joined him and shouted a few choice words after the old man.

The boys managed to retrieve the ball, but they also began to watch Golrup's every move, waiting for a chance to get back at him. Now, old man Golrup had a persistent problem: he suffered severe constipation. As a result, he spent long intervals on the pot. On one occasion, he sensed a signal from his bowels while on his way to the post office. There was a public restroom near the town square and he stopped there in hopes of relieving himself. It was a small restroom and that meant there was no room for his rollator. He had to leave it outside. Of course, he spent quite a long time inside. Men tried knocking on the door when they needed the facility, and he would simply growl at them to go away. This looked like an opportunity to the boys. When they heard the old man tell someone to go away, they knew this was the time for their revenge. They took the rollator and hid it behind a tool shed two blocks away. Then they took up positions along the way to watch him stumble about in search of his essential prop.

He did indeed stumble about to the delight of the boys. He could barely stand without the support of his rollator. He lurched this way and that. He almost fell to the ground, but saved himself by grabbing a tree branch. He could hear the boys snickering as they watched him and it made him so irate that he swung his fist around in the air with such force that he actually fell flat. This time he simply could not get up. The boys continued to mock and taunt him. Eventually, they dispersed one by one and left him lying in the dirt.

He lay there very still, breathing hard. Once in a while he struggled to get to his feet, but he always fell back. A few people went by and stopped to look, but no one offered to help. Then something strange happened. One of the boys came back. He stood beside the old man who turned to him with pitiful eyes.

"Say, Mister," said the boy. "I want to ask you something."

"What? What do you want to ask me, kid?"

The boy was quiet for a while. Then slowly he asked the old man if he really could not get up. "What do you think? Does it look like I can get up? You think I like lying in this dirt? Huh?"

"No," said the boy simply.

"Well?"

"Well, maybe I could help you."

"You? How could you possibly help me to my feet? You have some kind of super power?"

"Nope."

"What then?"

"I know something."

"Huh!" the old man snorted. "You know something. What do you know?"

"That whatcha-ma-call it, that thing with wheels you use to get around. I know where it is."

Golrup was silent. Then slowly and quietly he said, "Do you suppose you could go get it?"

"Yep. Wait here." Saying that, he ran off to the tool shed.

Golrup started chuckling. "Wait here," he says. He repeated that a couple of times and it got him to laughing outright. That was the first time in months, if not years, that Clarence P. Golrup IV had laughed.

The boy came back, awkwardly pushing the rollator. He placed it along side the old man who reached up to the handle with his right arm. The boy pulled up on the man's left arm and after many pulls and pushes, Golrup was upright. This time the boy laughed. It was a laugh of triumph.

The two of them stood together for a short while, just looking at each other until finally Golrup said, "Thanks, kid."

They each went on his way. Clarence P. Golrup IV learned something that day. Little by little he began to be corrigible. Indeed, someone observed him deliberately committing an act of civility.

The UGLY Half-Sister

COMES TO TOWN

*I*n the tiny town of Lower Piddlington, a beautiful young woman named Sofia caught the eye of the men about town, young and old. Wherever she would go, she attracted admiring stares, even whistles and catcalls from men who would gather in a tight knot. Sometimes one or two men would stop her, thinking they might engage her in suggestive conversation. She had a charming way of sidestepping them graciously and moving on. As you might expect, the gossiping ladies around town would clear their collective throat and invent all manner of scandalous adventures associated with the woman. They declared Sofia to be a loose woman, a shameless hussy, a jezebel, a harlot and worse. They invented vivid stories of her erotic adventures and they would huff and puff with righteous indignation. Seeing the men fall all over themselves to get Sofia's attention, the gossiping ladies would invent ever more outrageous stories about her.

None of this is surprising. At one time, the town of Lower Piddlington was notorious for its indulgence in petty vices such as envy, jealousy, cheating, and abusing one another's reputation. Nevertheless, it began to annoy Sofia. It came to a point that she determined to do something about it. She had lived in this town since her early teens when her father moved there after her mother died. In the span of those several years she had watched him deteriorate with mental degeneration. She decided whatever had to be done, she would have to do it herself.

She invented a half-sister and gave her the name of Letitia. She let it be known that Letitia was coming to visit. She went into great detail about her sheer beauty, describing her rich red hair, her full lips and flashing blue eyes. She discretely hinted at her shapely figure and the grace with which she walked. To conclude, she let it be known that Letitia would arrive in Lower Piddlington the very next day. Having whetted the curiosity of the gossiping ladies and the gaping men alike, she announced that the famous Letitia would be coming out for a walk about town the morning after she arrived.

Then she went about the task of making herself look grotesque. She put pads over her breasts, and one over her belly and two more over her hips. She applied makeup accentuating wrinkles and lumps and red cheeks and she blacked out a tooth. She pulled over her body a loud, red dress with gold braids and she topped it off with a carrot red tangled wig. She was a frightful sight to behold.

In anticipation of the passage of this wondrous goddess, men assembled just outside Sofia's house. Ladies practiced

THE UGLY HALF-SISTER COMES TO TOWN

discretion by scattering themselves at intervals along the pathway. They all expected to see the beautiful Sofia appear in the company of the even more beautiful Letitia. Of course, that did not happen. What did happen was the appearance of an astonishing monstrosity of a woman coming out of the house alone. This had a marvelous effect. The men scattered and the ladies pulled together. One of the men was a little too slow and Letitia (Sofia) caught up with him, wrapped her arms around him and pushed her cushioned self against him. He was aghast and the ladies were appalled. Then she turned her attention to the ladies who pulled together ever so tightly. She approached them and the closer she got, the more tightly they held onto one another. Then Sofia, in the person of Letitia, recited, in a hushed voice, bits of gossip about one lady after another. They, in turn, began to peel off, one by one. After a while, the whole group dispersed.

After that, Sofia (Letitia) strolled about the town while the townspeople peered at her from their windows or from side streets. Finally, Letitia went home. The next day, Sofia came out of the house to take her usual walk about town. She greeted her neighbors cheerfully. It took some time before anyone summoned up the courage to confront her with questions about her half-sister. They wanted to know why she wasn't with her yesterday, why she wasn't with her today and finally, of course, why she called that woman "beautiful". Sofia said nothing except to announce that Letitia had left early in the morning, preferring not to spend any more time in this town. From that day forward, however, the town of Lower Piddlington developed a new civility and women were ladies and the men, gentlemen. Sofia was pleased to pass the news to her half-sister, Letitia.

The *ANXIOUS* Page-Turner

Despite his youth, Cuthbert Perry was an accomplished pianist, playing with precision and feeling. He graduated from the conservatory with high recommendations and was looking forward to a career as a concert pianist in some of the most prestigious concert halls. There was a flaw in this plan: he suffered severe stage fright.

One of his very supportive teachers, Hilde Baumgartner, a highly respected musician from Vienna's Academy of Music, sought ways to cure the poor young man of his tendency to panic. For example, she would orient the piano pointing upstage, so that he would have his back to the audience as he played. Another scheme called for him to enter only after the house lights had gone down, leaving him facing such bright spotlights he could not see the audience. She even suggested that he enter the stage with his face averted from the auditorium. These measures met with modest success, but the anxiety still affected his performance.

One day, Maestro Antonio Benvenuti, a special friend of Hilde Baumgartner, came to town. People of Greater Piddlington

THE ANXIOUS PAGE-TURNER

boasted of the acoustics of their famous concert hall, and the board of directors had persuaded him to perform a concert of works of his choosing. He was noted for his magnificent recordings of Vivaldi's concerti and he chose to perform three concerti from "La Serenissima" for a new recording. Hilde hosted a reception for the famous musician and she made sure that Cuthbert had the chance to meet him. The Maestro was very much taken with this young man. He declared that he would be honored if Cuthbert would assist him as his Page Turner. With some slight trepidation, Cuthbert said it would be his honor to do so.

The next afternoon, preparations were underway. A technician saw to it that the piano was tuned and a crew put all the recording equipment in place. Cuthbert was given the score of the concerti to look over before the performance. At the appointed time, he took his place in the wings with Hilde and the Maestro. He could hear the murmuring of the crowd and the occasional laughs and coughs. While it made him nervous, he reassured himself that he was not on serious duty. Hilde went out on stage and made an eloquent introduction of her friend. To great applause, Antonio Benvenuti marched onto stage, followed meekly by young Cuthbert. Once the Maestro had elaborately adjusted his bench, Cuthbert took his position upstage of the piano, ready to turn the pages.

All went well with the first concerto and it elicited strong, enthusiastic applause. Well into the second concerto, something happened, something Cuthbert could not control. No matter how hard he tried, he could not stop the sneeze. It would have its way and it was a loud one. One could see that the Maestro was annoyed, but he did not break his stride and played on. Cuthbert was chagrined. He wanted to find his way into a hole.

While he was thinking about that hole, he suddenly realized the Maestro was coming to the end of the page. He jumped to attention, reached across and took the edge of the page. To his horror, he grabbed two pages and turned them. This time, the concert came to a stop. The Maestro could not carry on. Cuthbert bolted from the stage.

Hilde took over as page turner and the Maestro restarted the second concerto. The audience was pleased to hear it again. As for Cuthbert, he disappeared for several days running.

Cuthbert Perry put aside any ambition to go on the concert hall circuit. He became a stockbroker and insurance agent. From time to time he performed as a recording artist.

Following the concert, the Board of Directors hosted a reception in the foyer of the concert hall. Adoring audience members surrounded Antonio Benvenuti. Miss Baumgartner realized that Cuthbert had disappeared and she whispered to the Maestro that she was going to search for him. She knew Greater Piddlington and had some ideas where he might be found. Eventually she came on him seated on a bench in the city park. They sat silently for a long while. Then Cuthbert sobbed and blurted out, "I am so sorry!" She assured him that all had gone off well, as the audience even delighted in hearing the second concerto start over. She also told him that the Maestro did not want to leave town until he had a chance to talk with Cuthbert.

Miss Baumgartner ushered him back to the concert hall where the crowd had dispersed and Antonio was gathering his belongings. He smiled at Cuthbert and embraced him. He told him he must not torture himself over the incident of the page turn. He has too much to offer the world of music to let this stop him. The three of them talked a long while about his talent and also his panic before an audience. Antonio Benvenuti declared that he had an idea. He needed some time, but he would be back in touch.

After nearly three weeks, the Maestro had news and he invited Cuthbert to see him. He had rented, in Greater Piddlington, a recording studio equipped with a piano. He invited Cuthbert to play any piece he liked and it would be recorded. He chose a sonata by Domenico Scarlatti and he did it from memory, without a page turner. The recording was very successful. It led to a contract to create an album of all Scarlatti's piano sonatas. It led to other contracts. For all of them, he played wonderfully, but always in a studio without an audience.

THE TRANSFORMATION OF LUGUBRIOUS LOUIE

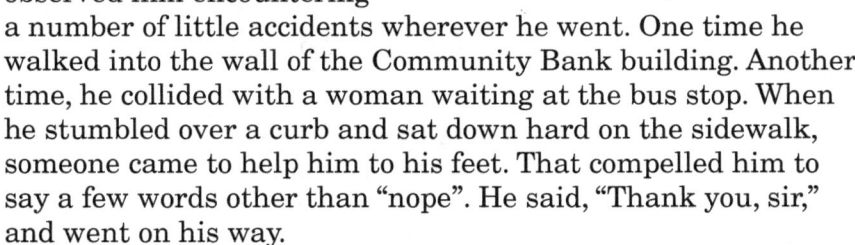

At first the good people of Lower Piddlington were unaware that a stranger had come to their town. Then they began to notice a man who plodded about, his shoulders sloped down and his head hanging low. He had a hangdog look about him and was a sort of Sad Sack. People tried to engage him in conversation, but he would look away. At most he only mumbled a single word, usually simply "Nope".

Naturally, that provoked a lot of talk in town. They observed him encountering a number of little accidents wherever he went. One time he walked into the wall of the Community Bank building. Another time, he collided with a woman waiting at the bus stop. When he stumbled over a curb and sat down hard on the sidewalk, someone came to help him to his feet. That compelled him to say a few words other than "nope". He said, "Thank you, sir," and went on his way.

One day, he went to his mail box at the post office. Looking through the circulars and advertisements, he came upon a check. It came from his previous landlord, reimbursing him for his apartment deposit. That put a slight smile on his face as he went to the Community Bank to open an account and deposit the money. As he walked along, admiring the check in his hand, a gust of wind tore it away and sent it flying, flitting and floating. He stumbled every which way, trying to catch up with it. Some passersby were amused watching him lurching about.

At last, the wind let up and the check began to settle toward the ground. Before it could land, Charlie Gunkle, the town bully, snatched it out of the air. Our Sad Sack was out of breath by the time he caught up with the check now in the hands of Charlie.

Charlie looked at the paper. "This appears to be a check."

"Yes. It's mine."

"Oh? Well, what's your name?"

"I'm Louie Benderbeck."

"Now this check is made out to a Louis Benderbeck."

"That's the same."

"No. One is Louis, the other is Louie. And you're Louie."

"I'm both."

"I'm gonna call you Louie the Loser. How 'bout that?" Saying that, Charlie, who was tall, held the check up high and forced Louie to jump for it. Finally, Charlie gave Louie the check and sauntered off, laughing and repeating "Louie the Loser" over and over.

Feeling sadder than ever, Louie took the check to the bank. He filled out the paper work to establish an account and put the money from the check in it. As he turned to leave the bank, a smiling gentleman stopped him, saying, "Do excuse me, may I introduce myself? I am Pastor Barttleby. I heard what Big Boy Charlie Gunkle said to you and I had a few choice words with him myself. You're no loser, but you do appear very sad."

THE TRANSFORMATION OF LUGUBRIOUS LOUIE

Louie was startled and could not think what to say. Finally he muttered, "Things never seem to go my way, but things are often in my way."

"Ah, well, you're not Louie the Loser. I shall call you Lugubrious. That's it. Lugubrious Louie." Then the man clapped him on the back and quoted a Bible verse: "May those who sow in tears reap with shouts of joy?" He smiled and left the bank.

Louie did not know quite what to make of that. He stood there in the bank foyer and shook his head. Then, he made his way homeward puzzling over "sowing in tears". Over the next few days, the epithet "Lugubrious Louie" circulated about town and people began calling him by that name. Louie accepted it for he did indeed feel lugubrious.

That was about to change. Just two days later, Lugubrious Louie did something that caused the whole town to sit up and take notice. It all began when he was shuffling along and came to a stop. Lying on the ground was a segment of fence with a sign warning all to stay away because of danger. The danger was clear enough: there was an open hole recently dug in the ground. It did no good that the fence and the sign were laying on the ground. So, Louie picked the fence up, thinking to place it in front of the hole where it belonged. Doing so, he heard a whimpering sound from down inside the hole.

Louie put the fence down and went to the edge of the hole. He peered in, asking, "Is someone down there?"

"Yes," came the weak reply. After a moment, the voice went on, "I'm stuck down here. I can't get out." It was the voice of a young girl.

Louie straightened his shoulders. He lay himself down on his stomach and thrust his arm down in the hole. "Can you take hold of my hand?"

"I can see it, but I can't reach it." The voice now turned to weeping quietly.

"Please, don't worry. We're going to get you out of there. Just hold on."

Louie was thinking fast. Could he find a ladder, perhaps? Or maybe a rope? He started to look around frantically. There were some tools left there by the workers. One was a long neck shovel. It had a big handle. "That might work," he thought. He went back to lying on his stomach at the edge of the hole. "Can you grab hold of this?" he asked, as he put the upside down shovel into the hole. "Yes," came the reply. "Grab hold with all your might. I'll pull you up." After a few moments Louie felt the shovel jump. "Oh, no! I lost my grip," cried the voice. "Try again, tighter, tighter!" he said.

By this time a small group had gathered, curious as to what Lugubrious Louie was doing lying on his stomach on the edge of the hole. Someone blurted out, "What in the world are you doing, lying by that hole?" Louie cried out, "You've got it! Hold on, Hold on! I'm pulling you up." And he did. Once he got the girl within reach, he caught hold of her and pulled her to safety on the ground. There, the two of them lay on the ground, catching their breath.

The people gathered around clapped their hands. A woman cried out, "Why, that's Clarissa Landescomb!" She ran to the child and held her in her arms. Louie looked around and saw that this child was weeping for joy. So were some of the other people. A gentleman helped Louie to his feet and clapped him on the back. He received a round of applause. Someone brought Clarissa's mother and again there was more weeping and clapping. Someone at the back of the crowd was heard to say, "You've reaped with shouts of joy."

From that day forward, Louie developed a perpetual smile and a spring in his step. He did, of course, continue to have his little accidents, but they no longer affected him. On those occasions when he met Pastor Barttleby on the street, he would repeat "Shouts of joy" and the Pastor would wink his right eye.

A Squabbling COUPLE

From time to time, the fourth floor apartment at 23 Polar Avenue, just two blocks from Lower Piddlington's main square, would explode and become a battlefield. The warfare was particularly noticeable in the spring and summer when the windows were open. People out for their evening strolls would stop to listen as the weapons were being fired. There were only two weapons creating all that tumult, but they were easily identified: one was a screeching soprano and the other, a growling bass. Growls sometimes rode over screeches, screeches sometimes over growls. There were also occasions when only one was firing, doing so in a kind of rising aria of unremitting ferocity. When that happened, it was usually followed by a long pause. During any such pause, strollers on the street were known to applaud. The performer never acknowledged it, being occupied in watching the other performer preparing to fire a rat-a-tat-tat volley of retorts. So the war went on in alternating arias and recitatives.

These battles were the creation of Wanda and Will Torrance, residents of Lower Piddlington for over ten years. Their squabbles sometimes turned into skirmishes, but they didn't usually last very long. In fact, they attracted little attention. Afterwards, one might meet Will muttering to himself as he walked to the Town Hall where he worked as a clerk. Or Wanda would come out stomping her feet in frustration as she went to her job as a loan officer for the Community Bank. The Hall and the Bank were both on the main square, but the couple never walked there together.

Little by little, in the evening, the voices of the performers grew in volume, especially with the advent of spring and the opening of windows. That was when audiences began to form in the street below. Suddenly, in the middle of April, a battle erupted, this time in the early morning. This was really loud and undeniably serious. Things had gotten to the point they could not wait until evening. They had at each other with a vengeance. A small crowd gathered in the street, and this time everyone could make out what they were saying.

It started with the growl of the bass voice: "Why don't you get dressed in the morning? You walk around wrapped in that ratty old terrycloth robe, your hair up in rollers. You couldn't be uglier. It's disgusting!"

"Well, it's nice to have an effect on someone, you old scarecrow. You're plenty ugly yourself, like a ragged bean stalk."

A SQUABBLING COUPLE

"I can't take much more of you! Why don't you go home to Momma?"

"Why should I go home to Momma? This is my house. You go home to your Momma, if she'd have you?"

"You know very well that my Momma is dead. Listen, you old sow. Your sagging mug is the first thing I see in the morning and the last I see every night. I need a new vista, one I can bear to look at."

"Ooo! I see. That new vista you talk about, is that the cute little thing with the bobbed hairdo and those freckled cheeks? The one who shakes her booty every time she passes your desk at the Town Hall? Could she be your new vista? Huh? Is she?"

At that point, the soprano stopped. There was a pause before she started up again.

"I'm right! I knew it. Trixie! That's her! Cute little bitch. Go shack up with her, why don't you? She'll throw off her sheets, open her legs, and give you a good vista. Go on! Go on! Get out of here." By that time, her voice was nearing full screech.

The growl of the bass took over. "You have no idea what you are talking about. You're making it all up. There is no Trixie."

"Oh, really? No Trixie?" Now at full screech: "Go! I never want to see you again. Ever!"

Then the crowd heard a door slam. Then all was quiet. Will Torrance emerged from the apartment building. At just that moment, Wanda appeared on the balcony and started throwing items to the ground. Will, poor fellow, had to scramble to gather it all – shaving kit, clock, a pair of shoes, a few books, two suits, many shirts, some trousers.

The soprano cried out from on high: "Here's a duffle bag for your stuff. Pack it all in and be on your way! Trixie's waiting." And she threw down that last item and slammed the balcony door. Will crawled around collecting his things. The audience began to disperse. Once the area was clear, Wanda came out of the apartment house and marched off to the Community Bank.

News of this last big squabble flew through the town. Those who weren't there to witness it wanted to hear all about it. In response, some actually magnified it and created ever bigger and better stories. At the bank, customers and clerks made a wide berth around Wanda who carried herself with dignified rage. At the Town Hall, where Will showed up for work, nobody knew quite what to say or do. They watched him as he tried to organize things out of the duffle bag.

As it happened, there was no Trixie. (Although there was a Peggy that Will liked to eye from time to time.) So there was no young woman waiting to take Will in. He'd have to register at the Hotel Excelsior and take an "extended stay" room.

After a few weeks, the town folks of Lower Piddlington spoke less and less about the squabbling couple. There was only so much to be said about the great war they waged at the last.

Then, one evening, Wanda appeared in the dining room of the Hotel Excelsior where Will sat having his supper. He was astonished to see her, the more so when she pulled up a chair and joined him at his table. He simply stared at her, waiting for her to say something. Finally, she did. She told him that she was leaving, going back to the town where they had lived ten years ago. She had her old job at the bank and she looked forward to rejoining that staff. She had cleared out of the apartment on Polar Avenue and she gave him the keys. Then she stood up as if to leave.

Will looked up at her: "Is that it? Is that all you have to say?"

"No. That is not it. There's something else. I just don't know how to say it."

"Well, have a seat. Give it a little time, maybe you'll figure it out. We have all evening in front of us."

She slowly returned to her chair. She took a deep breath. "I know there was no Trixie. But I didn't make her up. She came

A SQUABBLING COUPLE

from allusions you seemed to make to young women, implying that you had relationships. You didn't say it to me, but I heard you boast to your friends. It hurt. That is how our squabbling began."

Will thought about that a while and then said, "You're probably right – I created Trixie – sort of my dream girl."

"You thought about her a lot."

"Yeah, I guess I did."

"I know. I could tell."

The two sat silently for a while, just staring into space.

Wanda turned her gaze on him. "You know, we had an awful marriage."

He turned to her. "A really rotten marriage."

"Just terrible!" For several moments they stared at each other until she began to titter. Startled, Will began to chuckle. Then she began laugh and he joined in until they both were guffawing. People at other tables put down their knives and forks. They listened in amazement to that big guffaw that would renew itself every time it started to fade.

When at last the laughter fizzled out, Wanda stood up. "That is the only good laugh we've had out of our bad marriage. So much for marriage! Let's not do it anymore."

She turned to leave, then stopped. "Goodbye, Will. Maybe you'll find a real Trixie." She leaned down and kissed him on the forehead and left the dining room. Everyone returned to his or her meal, muttering and whispering about this strange development. What they did not notice was that Wanda had gone to the ladies' room, locked herself in a cubicle and wept. Nor did they hear Will's stifled sobs as he sat alone at his table.

The Town of BABEL

THE TOWN OF BABEL

*F*or nearly two decades, Max Welbourne served as Chairman of the Town Council of the village of Lower Piddlington. It was not a demanding job. The council met only once a month and the agenda was rarely extensive and almost never controversial. Moreover, Mr. Welbourne was an amiable fellow and the townspeople certainly did not envy him his position. Everyone was content to have him take the responsibility of organizing and chairing the committee. Whenever his two-year term was up, people urged him to run again and no one came forward to challenge him. So it was that one day in late October, he won another term by a landslide vote. The incumbent members of the council also kept their seats.

The townspeople were not only pleased with these results, they organized a parade through the streets of Lower Piddlington featuring the high school band, police riding on horses, a few classic cars, and two floats left over from the high school homecoming. Seated on a throne high atop the second float was Geoffrey Bolton, Mayor of Greater Piddlington (a man of some girth) holding his outstretched arms in triumph. Following that float was an open convertible in which Max Welbourne rode, waving to the happy crowd. The parade entered the central square and came to a stop at the Town Hall. The council members were there to greet the Mayor (who required assistance to get down from his throne) and the Chairman.

The officials and many citizens went straight into the Council Chamber for the ceremonial opening of the new term. Each council member presented his or her credentials and the secretary administered the oath of office for the members and the Chairman. After that, Mayor Bolton lumbered up to the podium, spread out his papers and launched into a long speech on the liberties and responsibilities that attend upon serving the community, whether as elected officer or as simple citizen. People knew when to clap, having heard these words before.

At the end of all these rituals and the Mayor's speech, it was Max's obligation to end the program with a few last words. He used them to encourage the Council to be alert and responsive to issues that may arise during their tenure. He spoke in his usual quiet and unassuming tone that had always earned him the approval and applause of the audience. He ended his talk with these words: "Let me assure you that I will put forth every effort to assume the duties of my office with integrity, honesty and forthrightness. Let me just add, in the spirit of good will, zeb nirtollow quadniss mir. Myoke digh morribby cate fow. Moidre babado!" With that, he smiled broadly and held up his arms as expression of acceptance. His smile faded and his arms dropped. He expected applause but instead saw blank faces. People seemed puzzled as they rose from their seats. He was more puzzled than anyone.

As always, the crowd adjourned to the ballroom of the Hotel Excelsior for a reception organized by Miss Margaret Murchison. She had always been regarded as a sort of a dowager duchess. In fact, people spoke of her as Lady Margaret, sponsor of all town social events. She basked in the town's adulation.

Lady Margaret was also very fond of Max Welbourne. They were, in fact, very close friends. They often sought each other out and shared jokes and gossip. Moreover, they gave each other whatever support the situation called for. On this occasion, she felt Max definitely needed support. Something was wrong. Once people had found their finger food and cups of punch, she took him aside: "What in the world is wrong with you?"

"What in the world <u>should</u> be wrong with me?"

"Don't you realize that you were spouting gibberish at the end of your speech?"

"I was not."

"You were! Tell me, what does 'Moidre babado' mean?"

"How am I supposed to know?"

"That's what you said. I distinctly recall your saying 'moidre babado' after you had said many other nonsensical words. Do you deny it?"

THE TOWN OF BABEL

"I most certainly do. I have no idea what 'moidre babado' means. How could I have said such a thing?"

"What do you think you said at the end of your speech?"

"Oh, something about my gratitude for the support, good nature and civility I find in this town -- and I added my best wishes."

"Aha! 'Best wishes.' That is what 'moidre babado' means!"

Max stared blankly at Lady Margaret. Then he shrugged and walked off in search of a pimento cheese sandwich and a cup of punch.

Some time later, as people were mingling with one another, Lady Margaret brought a young man to Max and introduced him, saying, "This is Jeremy Cogdon, a new resident in our village. Jeremy, meet Max Welbourne, Chairman of the Town Council."

The two of them got to talking about the reason Jeremy had come to town and about how Max could be of service as he settles in. In the course of their conversation, Max laughed and said, "Now that reminds me of a joke." Jeremy encouraged him to tell it. As he began to tell the joke, people gathered around listening.

Max took a breath and began: "Gaquel torme tallioregy abo, yepseehepzox nea' abo terigim ras, 'Yo digga nearo?' 'Digga maia billowad nof.' Aber so layly bousnix. 'Ah, cerripish noynay birrte nack'!" Jeremy burst out in laughter, saying, "Nessibow tress hoat! Yoya hibel met! Bloa bloa!" The young man was almost doubled over in laughter.

"Wait, wait!' called Lady Margaret. "Just a minute. Jeremy Cogdon – you understood what Max was saying?"

"What is there to understand? It's just a joke," said Max.

"But it was all gibberish! Absolute nonsense! And then, here's Jeremy understanding that gobbledygook. How do you know those words?"

31

Jeremy was trying to get his breath and finally managed to say, "Those words are just plain English. Of course I know them."

Max and Jeremy looked at each other. This was beginning to look very strange. They both thought they were speaking English, but others heard gibberish. They could not control what others heard. What's more, they had nothing to do with shifting into or out of what Lady Margaret was calling gibberish. It just happened.

Much murmuring filled the Excelsior ballroom. After a while, people began to talk, some in English, some in gibberish. They became more and more alarmed. They had no control over what was going to come out of their mouths. Some understood the gibberish and some answered with like words. The chatter grew louder and louder, more and more frantic – a true cacophony.

Mayor Bolton held up his arms and demanded quiet. He had to shout two or three times before the crowd calmed down. Taking a chance that what he was about to say could slip into gibberish, he began a speech: "Citizens, ladies and gentlemen, you must not let panic take over. Yes, what is happening here is alarming and mysterious, but it won't help if you allow yourselves to be caught up in fear. Now, let us all quietly go on our way to our respective homes. We'll find our way through this, I promise."

Gradually, the ballroom emptied and people dispersed. Max walked with Mayor Bolton to his car where they conferred. The Mayor declared his intention to appoint a small group of experts in various fields and send them to Lower Piddlington to find the source of this phenomenon. Then he got in his car and drove off toward Greater Piddlington.

In the days that followed, there were more instances of gibberish working its way into conversations. People became reticent about speaking with one another for fear it would turn into gibberish. The town became quiet and still.

Keeping his word, the Mayor sent a group of scientists to investigate. Among them were a linguist, a psychologist, and a physiologist. Two were from the Department of Health and Community Services. They went straight to work doing language tests, examinations of the mouth, throat and lungs, and the cognitive functions of the brain. They even tested the drinking water. They did interviews and sought out what common factors were present when the gibberish showed up.

They finally came to the conclusion that the origin of this social malady was a rare and poorly understood virus that settles in that portion of the brain that controls reason and language, causing random alternation between English and gibberish. It is an epidemic that simply has to run its course. There is no vaccine to prevent it in the future. For a while, it disrupted Town Council meetings by turning well-considered speeches into nonsense. But at the end of the fifth week, it disappeared, and every conversation reverted to clear English. It was over.

Everyone hoped the gibberish virus would never return. Townspeople felt a renewed sense of unity and civility. Max Welbourne was relieved but he also decided he would not run for another term as the Chairman of the Town Council. Lady Margaret reluctantly approved his decision. People swore they would never forget that weird October reception at the Excelsior when their community became the Town of Babel.

A *Doomsayer* Marches *in The Streets*

O ne afternoon in early June, a strange and disheveled man showed up marching through the city of Greater Piddlington. As he marched, his flowing ragged clothes fluttering behind him, he declared his warning. He was shouting it over and over: "THE ENDTIME IS UPON US. NOW IS THE

A DOOMSAYER MARCHES IN THE STREETS

TIME TO REPENT. REPENT WHILE YOU STILL MAY."
No one knew who he was or where he came from. He simply appeared. They made way for him as if his ferocity pushed them aside.

He went the length of the main street and out the town gate. He descended the steep paths and entered the village of Lower Piddlington. He went straight to the town square, shouting the same message. Sofia threw open her window to see what was happening, as did Margaret Murchison, also known as Lady Margaret. Out on the street, some townspeople, such as Cuthbert Perry and Jerry Cogdon, stood back, alarmed, and let this stranger storm ahead, still shouting his warning. He almost pushed Hilde Baumgartner aside. When he was about to enter the central square, he came to a stop, his path blocked by Clarence P. Golrup IV, the town curmudgeon, standing with his rollator and challenging the man to continue his march. They stood there, face-to-face, unmoving for some time. Then the man broke the spell with a grand proclamation that he was doing God's holy work and he offered to give Golrup a whack with his walking stick. Golrup yielded and the man continued his march through the square and out of town.

The next day and the day after, the man appeared with the same march and the same shouts of warning. This time Golrup stayed out of his way. These warnings were a little more elaborate and frightening with images of the galloping horses of the Apocalypse, the horrors of the battle of Armageddon and the Mark of the Beast. People were beginning to think there ought to be a way to drive him out of town or at least shut the man up. A group visited with Pastor Barttleby, thinking that an exorcism might bring a halt to this madness. The Pastor was dubious. Another group called on Max Welbourne, Chairman of the Town Council, to convene the members and develop a plan of action.

It all became more urgent on the fourth day. The man appeared with descriptions of the disasters awaiting people in the coming turbulence of the Great Tribulation, which will bring intense storms, famines, earthquakes, wildfires, murder and mayhem.

Anxiety began to seize the minds of the citizens of both Lower and Greater Piddlington. Some became anxious that the man's predictions of horrors and disasters were about to come true. Others were simply concerned about the annoyance of having this man around spouting descriptions of one cataclysmic event after another. They just wanted him to go away. Everybody wondered where he was staying that he could show up every day to torment people. Whatever the case, Max Welbourne called the members of the Council together. They agreed that the man should be located and that an effort to stop him be made in tandem with Mayor Geoffrey Bolton and the City Board of Greater Piddlington.

On the fifth day, he came through with ever more images of the pain and suffering that was about to be inflicted on the good people of the Piddlington towns. Golrup was out on the street and glared at the man as he passed by. Then he heard a little voice calling, "Say, mister. You remember me?"

Golrup turned and saw the boy who had helped him get on his feet and brought him his rollator. "Oh, hey there, kid. You all right?"

"I betcha I know something you don't know."

"I bet you want to tell me something that you know that I don't know."

"Yep."

Golrup shuffled over to a park bench and motioned to the boy to sit with him. "Now, kid. First of all, what's your name? And then tell me what you know."

Feeling somewhat important, the boy settled on the bench. "My name is Ralph, Ralph Morse. What I know is about that man who just walked by, the one you were watching."

"OK. What do you know about that crazy man?"

"I know where he lives."

"There are many people who would like to know that. How do you know?"

A DOOMSAYER MARCHES IN THE STREETS

"Well, see, I like to hike around all those hills up above us. I found a cliff up beyond Greater Piddlington. There's a cave in that cliff. You can't see it very well except from the top of the next hill. Anyway, that's where that ragged old man lives. Inside that cave."

"You saw him?"

"Yep. Saw him go into it and saw him come out of it. Twice."

"He didn't see you?"

"Nope."

Golrup pondered this news. "What you know, Ralph, is pretty important -- so important that important people need to know it."

Before long many people knew about the cave. Geoffrey Bolton, Mayor of Greater Piddlington, responded to the request from the Council and called a joint meeting of the Town Council and the City Board.

Before that meeting could take place, the man showed up for the sixth day, declaring that the beginning of the end was nigh. The Great Tribulation will produce some horrendous event the very next day. Everyone needed to go for shelter and pray for forgiveness and salvation. There was no time left.

That same afternoon, the joint meeting was gaveled to order in a large chamber of the City Government Building. The place was packed with audience members, including, among others, the beautiful Sofia, the pianist Cuthbert Perry, the pastor Barttleby, as well as Jeremy Cogdon and Lady Margaret. Even the town bully, Charlie Gunkle, was there. Mayor Bolton announced the one item on the agenda which was to decide what, if anything, should be done about the disturbance the wild man creates in the two communities. Some argued that nothing should be done. He will go away after a while, and the right to speak freely is fundamental to society. Others declared that freedom of speech cannot apply when language is used to undermine social cohesion, and that the man is dangerous and must be stopped. A member of the Council moved that a small

37

three-person committee be formed and empowered to develop contingency plans if the man refuses to stop. Should that be the case, the man must be arrested and charged with disturbing the peace. With that in mind, the Sheriff should be ordered to stand by.

There remained a problem. Where was the man? Everyone had heard he was in a cave but no one knew where that cave was, not even Clarence Golrup. Mayor Bolton called the Morse household. Mrs. Morse answered and the Mayor explained that her young son, Ralph, was needed to lead the way to the cave where the wild man lived. She was startled. Ralph had never told her about a cave. She knew he liked to go for long walks and she asked if the Mayor knew the general whereabouts of this cave.

Mayor Bolton took in a deep breath. "Well, madam, we know it is somewhere north of Greater Piddlington, but only Ralph knows exactly where. We need to speak with this wild man. We need Ralph to show us the way to the man's cave."

Mrs. Morse was shocked. "I had no idea he hiked so far from home. Did he meet that awful man?"

"No, I don't believe so. He said he saw him going in and out of the cave, but the man never saw him. With your permission, madam, we would like Ralph to meet the County Sheriff at the town square at two o'clock this afternoon. The Sheriff will drive him up to the area north of Greater Piddlington. From there, Ralph can lead the Sheriff and his men to the vicinity of the cave. We really do need his help."

Mrs. Morse was flabbergasted. It took a while before she could say anything. She thought of the Great Tribulation that was to start today. She put that out of her mind and said, "Well, I guess it would be all right if he will be with the Sheriff. I'll tell him."

After the phone call, the Mayor appointed the three persons to serve on the planning committee. A short time later, the Sheriff and his two deputies met Ralph at the town square and drove

A DOOMSAYER MARCHES IN THE STREETS

to a convenient spot to start the trek to the cave. Ralph led the way up to the crest of a hill. From there, the cave was visible. Then he took them down into a deep ravine and up to the mouth of the cave. The Sheriff went ahead. He bent down and called into the darkness, "Hullo, hullo, anybody home?"

A voice boomed out of the depths, "NO. GO AWAY." The force of the reply rocked the group back on their heels. Of course, they did recognize that voice as the one they heard so often shouting dire warnings in the streets of their communities.

The Sheriff stepped forward again. "Sir, we mean no disrespect. We just wish to speak with you. Please come out where we can see you."

Again the voice came back. "NO. GO AWAY."

"This is the Sheriff speaking. We are concerned about the disturbance you create by going through our streets, shouting and upsetting everyone. We are asking you to cease and desist. I need you to understand that if you choose to ignore our request for your cooperation, I will have no choice but to arrest you."

Again: "NO. GO AWAY."

The Sheriff motioned to the deputies and the three prepared to enter the cave, one of them pulling out handcuffs and the other two bringing out their guns. Having made themselves ready for the worst, they started into the cave. Before they got very far, they came back out, as if forced by the wild man emerging from the depths.

"What is wrong with you people?" he shouted. "Haven't I told you again and again that the end is here? It's now. Today. The Great Tribulation will begin this very day. I am sheltering in my place. Get away from here and find your own shelter. GO AWAY." He turned to go back into the cave.

The Sheriff called after him. "We only want a simple promise from you. If we have that promise, we will go away. Will you cease and desist your practice of marching through our streets shouting warnings? That is all."

The man stopped and looked at him. "Are you stupid? After today I won't be here. Neither will you. Nor will your town. The whole earth will be taken up. So prepare yourselves. With prayer and repentance, you may be taken up in the Rapture. You're running out of time." With that he turned again and went into the depths of his cave.

Those left behind shook their heads. "Rapture?" they wondered. There seemed nothing more to be done there. Ralph led them back to the starting place. The Mayor met them and asked what had happened. When the Sheriff told him, he, too, shook his head and said "Rapture?"

People asked Pastor Barttleby if they had anything to fear. The good pastor smiled and said, "No. Not a thing. The man has it all wrong, mixing up the Rapture and the Tribulation and neither one is today."

From that day forward, nobody got more than a glimpse of the wild man. He continued to live in his very own cave, waiting for another holy message. For the people, there remained a nagging worry, a fear that it will all start over again some day. He could come again marching down the streets and shouting dire warnings. They said it could happen any time. It never did. Eventually, people realized he was no longer there. He had somehow disappeared as mysteriously as he had appeared. Someone remarked that he may have been caught up in the Rapture.

A Wedding & A Funeral

THE CHRONICLES OF LOWER PIDDLINGTON

Several years passed after the Doomsayer marched the streets of the two Piddlingtons. It was an episode no one could forget and one they all hoped would never happen again. That madman was gone and people said "good riddance". They also said that they would not wish that affliction on any other town.

The good folks of Lower Piddlington got on with their lives. Louie Benderbeck (no longer lugubrious) opened a store stocked with a delightful range of children's toys. He also formed a close bond with Clarissa Landescomb, whom he had rescued from that deep hole so many years earlier. He thought of her as his daughter. In somewhat similar fashion, Maestro Benvenuti coached, taught, and sponsored Cuthbert Perry with such success that he returned to Greater Piddlington and gave a live performance in the concert hall, to the absolute delight of Miss Baumgartner. To this must be added the good cheer the old curmudgeon Clarence P. Golrup IV brought to the town. He was no longer quite so cantankerous and he did, on occasion, allow his crusty face to split into a smile. He took on an avuncular role in the life of young Ralph Morse who had helped him when he could not get up.

Ralph graduated from the State University. In the fall he would begin his new job teaching fifth graders at the local elementary school. The biggest news shared all over Lower Piddlington was about him. People had noticed, in a quiet sort of way, that he had fallen in love with Clarissa Landescomb and she with him. No one challenged the rumor that the two were planning to wed. Yet, while the news persisted, they themselves hadn't made such plans.

One afternoon, the two were cuddling in the huge recliner chair in the Landescomb drawing room. At first it was simply pleasant, but after a time it became exciting. Suddenly, Clarissa pulled away and prompted this very romantic conversation:

"You know what the people in the village say about us?"

Ralph thought for a moment. "What DO the people in the village say about us?"

A WEDDING & A FUNERAL

"They say we're planning to get married."

"Ah!" He smiled.

"Well? Are we?"

"No, but I think it sounds like a good idea."

"Do you? Is that a proposal?" She was about to hit him with a little pillow.

"Yes. Yes, that's a proposal. Let's get married."

"That's no proposal. Get down on your knee and do it right." And she playfully pushed him off the chair.

He very obligingly went down on his knee at the base of that huge chair and pronounced these words: "Clarissa, dear Clarissa, dearest Clarissa Landescomb, please tell me. May I have the honor of hearing your consent to be my wife?"

"Yes! I thought you'd never ask."

Just then, the door of the drawing room was thrown open and Mr. Landescomb came in. He stopped in mid-stride and said, "Sir, seeing you in that awkward position makes me think you have designs on my daughter. Is that so?"

Ralph got to his feet and stammered, "Yes, yes. I do. I have designs of making her my wife, sir. With your blessing, of course, sir."

Before he could answer, Mrs. Landescomb came into the room. She looked at the couple, now standing up next to one another. She clapped her hands together and declared, "Oh, Ralph! How wonderful! Welcome to our family!" And she went and embraced him and then Clarissa. She stood back admiring them. Then she said, "We must have a party to celebrate along with Mr. and Mrs. Morse." Then she remembered that Mr. Morse had died five years ago. "Do forgive me, Ralph."

"Still, this calls for a toast!" Mr. Landescomb bolted from the room and returned with a champagne bottle, already cooling in an ice bucket, and four flutes. So it was that Miss Clarissa Landescomb became officially engaged to Mr. Ralph Morse.

In the days and weeks that followed, elaborate plans were being laid for the great event. Margaret Murchison (aka, Lady Margaret) insisted on hosting the wedding reception in the ballroom of the Hotel Excelsior and she consulted with Mrs. Landescomb and Mrs. Morse on all the arrangements. Lady Margaret held a permanent position, one might say, as Socialite Designate, almost a royal appointment. Clarissa was caught up in a flurry of bridal showers. She and Ralph met with Pastor Barttleby for marital counseling. The ladies of the church gave Clarissa hints on her part in the ceremony.

Meanwhile, Ralph spent some time with his friend and honorary uncle, Clarence Golrup. He wanted him to be a part of the wedding party, and in fact to stand up as his Best Man. Clarence was pleased to be involved, but he said he only hoped his health would stay with him until the appointed day.

Just three days before the wedding, Ralph was walking toward the central square. As he approached the municipal rest room building, he saw a man lying on the ground next to a rollator. He shook his head, thinking that he was having a dream. It was not a dream. It was Clarence at the exact same spot where the boy (Ralph) had helped him so many years ago. Ralph stopped still in his tracks.

Then he ran to Clarence. "Here I am. It's me, Ralph. I'll get your rollator and help you get to your feet." He got the rollator and brought it next to the man. "Now we'll do it together just as we did before, only I'm stronger now. Give me your arm."

"No, Ralph. No. It's no use. I don't have the strength. My time is up, Ralph. I'm dying."

"No, you're not. I'll get help." Ralph ran off to the public telephone. He called the emergency number and came back to sit with Clarence. It took a while for the ambulance to arrive, as it had to come from the regional hospital in Greater Piddlington.

While they waited, Clarence summoned up enough breath to give Ralph some important instructions. He started by apologizing, "Dear boy, I really am dying. I know it. It makes me sad not to be with you at your wedding. Please think of me as if I were right there beside you." He let his head roll back before he could continue. "You need to know that I have made the necessary arrangements with the funeral home and with Pastor Barttleby. Please contact them when it's time to schedule…Oh, I want you to go to the law office of Max Welbourne…" At that point he ran out of energy.

The ambulance arrived and Ralph watched as the attendants put Clarence onto a gurney. He was not allowed to ride with him and he was left there with the old rollator. He took it with him and went home. He got word shortly after: Clarence had died on the way to the hospital.

At home, he thought about death, about how it had taken his father from him five years ago and now had taken his friend. That friend had become a sort of surrogate father. As his mind roamed through experiences out of the past, he began to weep and the weeping led to sobs that convulsed his body. In the midst of that, the telephone rang. He let it ring while he regained composure. It was Clarissa. She insisted that she needed to be with him.

He went to her, grateful that she was there. When he arrived, she took him in her arms for a long embrace. They settled in that great chair and cuddled. For a while they said nothing. The quiet itself was soothing. Then slowly and very gently, Clarissa began to speak, first about how much that old grump meant to him. The phrase "old grump" caused them to laugh. He really was a grouch, but Ralph, more than anyone else, had brought him out of himself. She knew the man was grateful for that and she knew he valued the joy coming from their love.

For his part, Ralph knew she was right. The way to honor Clarence in his death is to experience the joy he wanted for them. She had managed to console him. He announced that he needed to speak with the Pastor. He stood. They embraced and kissed and he left with a new vigor.

That vigor began to transform itself as he walked through the streets on his way to the church. Grief can act like an ocean wave building higher and higher and then crashing over one's spirit. By the time he arrived at the Pastor's office he had become irrational. He declared vehemently that he wanted his Best Man with him by the altar even if he would be in his coffin.

Pastor smiled, "You mean you still want him to stand up with you?"

"Yes! That's exactly what I mean."

"In his coffin?' It was all Pastor Barttleby could do to keep from laughing. "To stand up with you, I guess we'll set the coffin in an upright position next to you."

Ralph stared at him. Pastor stared at Ralph. There was a pause. Pastor could contain himself no longer. Laughter bubbled up from deep within and burst forth. Between gasps he described the scene: "Then when the time comes…haha. When it's the moment for you…haha…to turn to Clarissa…why then the lid of the coffin opens and the corpse…haha…hands you the wedding ring. Hahaha…" Pastor was now rolling in his chair.

Ralph stared at the laughing man. The image of the lid opening and a scrawny hand emerging with the ring began to play in his mind and soon he too could not hold back laughter. After a while the whole office reverberated with laughter. It would die down and suddenly burst forth again. By the end, both men were weeping tears of mirth.

Wiping his eyes, Pastor Barttleby remarked that he hadn't had such a healthy laugh for a long time. Then he added, "We both know the power of grief. It can come upon us without warning. You and I have found that we have an opposing power that can lead into joy. You have found love and it brings a joy that your friend Clarence would never want to deny you." Ralph nodded.

They looked at each other and the laughter threatened to arise again. They kept it under control.

The day came. Ralph took his spot alone by the altar. When Ralph looked out over the crowd and saw so many dear friends, it put a smile on his face. Then, when he saw Mr. Landescomb escorting Clarissa toward him, new tears came to his eyes, this time tears of happiness. There were more such tears when he lifted the veil to reveal Clarissa's beautiful face.

Lady Margaret lived up to her reputation. The reception she organized at the Hotel Excelsior took on an atmosphere of energetic joy. The music, the dancing and the speeches all contributed to the spirit of celebration. Louie Benderbeck spoke lovingly of the bride, his sometime daughter, and Mr. Landescomb had much the same to say about the bride, who really was his daughter. Then, surprisingly, Max Welbourn, lawyer and former Chairman of the Town Council, made an announcement: "I have here on this paper some words given me by Clarence Golrup a few days before he passed. He asked me to read it to you. He writes: 'If circumstances should prevent me from being there to share in the delight and sheer happiness of these two wonderful young people, please know I am with you in spirit. People die, yes, but you cannot erase them. I have died but I am still there.'" At the end of the reception, Mr. Welbourn took Ralph aside and asked him to come to his office as he had papers to share with him, including the Last Will and Testament of Mr. Golrup. It seemed Ralph Morse would inherit more than a used rollator.

Last rites for Clarence P. Golrup IV were conducted five days later and many of the same people were there as had been there for the wedding.

THE CHRONICLES OF LOWER PIDDLINGTON

*The one-time curmudgeon gazes down
on his former hometown*

www.ingramcontent.com/pod-product-compliance
Lightning Source LLC
Chambersburg PA
CBHW071243090426
42736CB00014B/3200